FRENCH CATHEDRAL WINDOWS
of the
Twelfth and Thirteenth Centuries

DATE DUE

		Withdrawn	
MY 8 5			
OC 9 '85			
OC 28 '88			
AP 3 '90			
▪			
GAYLORD			PRINTED IN U.S.A.

FRENCH CATHEDRAL WINDOWS

OF THE TWELFTH AND THIRTEENTH CENTURIES

19 PLATES IN TWELVE COLORS DIRECT FROM THE ORIGINALS

Introduction by
MARCEL AUBERT

IRIS BOOKS

OXFORD UNIVERSITY PRESS

NEW YORK TORONTO

THE IRIS BOOKS ARE PRODUCED
under the direction of
DR. H. ZBINDEN (BERNE)
SWITZERLAND

Copyright (plates and text) by IRIS VERLAG BERNE
Printed in Switzerland 1947

Swiss Edition published by IRIS VERLAG, BERNE
Edition for France published by LIBRAIRIE PLON, PARIS

THE plates shown here reproduce as accurately as possible some twelfth and thirteenth century stained glass windows, selected from among the handsomest in a few of the cathedrals richest in glass of this period: Chartres, Le Mans, Poitiers, Sens and Bourges. No attempt is made to describe in detail all the characteristics of twelfth and thirteenth century cathedral windows, still less to furnish an inventory of them. The aim has been simply to show, through typical examples, the exceptional artistic merit of these windows with regard both to color and composition, and to indicate how stained glass evolved in form, design and coloration, while the technique remained the same.

The stained glass window of the period is a mosaic in glass. Every change in color is represented by an individual fragment of glass, and it is to this technique itself, as well as to the quality of glass used and the ability of the glass-painters, that these windows owe their incomparable richness.

The monk Theophilus, who lived in Germany at the beginning of the twelfth century, gives us the formula for making glass: two parts ash of beechwood or fern, yielding potash, an alkaline base, and one part river sand, washed free of earthy particles. M. Chesnau, in his analyses of ancient glass, has detected a little soda, due to a small amount of ocean salt having been added to the mixture, which reduced the transparency of the glass but made it more fusible and ductile. The use of ferruginous sand charged with alumina accounts for the resistance of this old glass, as shown by Léon Appert, and also for its very fine greenish tone.

Theophilus explains that when the glass mixture is fused for a long time it assumes a rather warm purplish cast, due to the presence of manganese in the ashes of the plants used; this is what he calls 'flesh-color.' To obtain the other colors, he advises grinding up glass cubes coming from antique mosaics. (This method, if used at all, could not have lasted long, for the source of supply would have been quickly exhausted.)

Suger, abbot of St. Denis, claims to have ground up sapphires in order to obtain the blue coloring of his panes. That no trace of this practice has been discovered is easily understood when one realizes that, apart from the very high cost of sapphires, which would have rendered their use impracticable, their power of coloration is negligible. The same can be said of lapis-lazuli, and of the lazulites, which are ultramarines and would not give the blue desired.

Glass was colored in the mass by metallic oxides added to the molten mixture while in process of fusion. The colors were few: blue, red, purple, green, and yellow.

Blue was obtained from an oxide of cobalt coming almost exclusively from mineral ores in Bohemia, and especially, according to M. Chesnau, from Schneeberg in Saxony. Very pure and plentiful during the twelfth century, it yielded a beautiful azure blue, which in the thirteenth century was often turned

5

to violet due to the presence of oxide of manganese, or was restored to a slightly greenish hue by means of copper dioxide.

Red, the result of cupric oxide,—obtained from copper filings thrown into the mixture along with a reduction agent, generally flaked iron,—was the most difficult color to handle if one was to attain during the process of fusion the magnificent tones desired. These reds were so rich and intense that light could not penetrate the entire thickness of the glass, and the use of the color had to be restricted to a thin red film plated onto clear glass, or else to a series of successive red strata, alternating with the uncolored paste which produced a veined effect in the mass of glass. In spite of claims to the contrary, ancient glass-makers never mixed gold with their glass paste in order to give greater brilliance to their reds.

Green comes from copper dioxide; it is sometimes tinged slightly blue by adding oxide of cobalt. Purple is oxide of manganese brought to its maximum degree of oxidation and mixed with a little iron oxide plus traces of copper, which are generally found together in manganese ores. As for yellow, Theophilus' prescription, a mixture of sulphur and coal, was apparently not used, and the color is usually obtained by adding sesquioxide of iron or dioxide of manganese. All these oxides, with the exception of cobalt, are to be found in the natural ores of France.

The beauty of the tones was further enhanced by the expert harmonization of color.

The glass originally was made at the building site, but in those large workshops where consumption was greatest it soon became necessary to lay in supplies from the glass-workers, whose furnaces were often to be found at the forest's edge. The stained windows were made on the site, doubtless by workshops which moved from town to town as fast as orders were received. In this way it was possible to judge on the spot what colors were to be used—according to whether the window to be paned faced north, south, east, or west, whether it opened on the sky or was shaded by a buttress, a part of the wall, a tower, or some outside structure, and according to whether it lit a dark or bright, a white or colored part of the church's interior. Moreover, the color intensity was regulated in relation to adjoining windows. At Chartres, the windows of the north side contain more blue, those of the south more red and orange; several of the lower windows where the lighting is dim are decorated in *grisaille*. The glass-painters of the Middle Ages, realizing the difference between painting on glass and regular painting, did not try to reconcile the one technique with the other. They knew that colors painted on glass have only a relative value, and affect each other much more than colors painted on opaque substances: red next to blue turns violet, a streak of white alongside of blue appears grayish or greenish, blue next to yellow becomes turquoise, while next to red it takes on an azure hue; red near yellow is orange, and the yellow turns into gold; complementary colors, when juxtaposed, serve to heighten each other. The radiation of certain colors is such that their tone, intensity, and appearance become modified in accordance with the degree of exterior lighting; Viollet-le-Duc has given some striking examples of this in his *Dictionary*. The radiation of blue is such that it dominates all other colors: it is the illuminant of the stained glass window, and glows both in gray and sunny weather; it frequently forms the background of a composition, and even when the background is red, blue never fails to give the window its brilliancy.

When the glass had been fused at red-heat in large fireproof clay pots and then colored by means of metallic oxides, the work of glass-blowing began.

There were two processes, the one producing cylinder or 'sheet' glass, the other 'crown' glass. In the first case, the workman gathers onto the tip of his blowing-tube some glass which is being fused in the crucible and shapes the mass on a marble slab; he blows until he achieves a cylinder, cuts it off at both ends and opens it along its axis with a piece of iron, then reheats and spreads out the glass with the help of tongs. In the second process, he blows the glass into a flattened sphere, fastens an iron rod called the 'punty' onto the side opposite the blowing-tube, breaks off the tube and widens the opening thus obtained by turning the glass rapidly in front of the furnace. Centrifugal force slowly opens up the spheroid, which becomes a plate from 40 to 60 centimeters in diameter, thicker at the center than at the sides. This difference in thickness, causing a greater or lesser intensity of color, was very ably used by the glass-painters to obtain color gradations and to relieve the monotony of the backgrounds.

Glass made this way is from 2 to 3 millimeters thick, with swellings up to 6 millimeters, especially when it is made in crown form and is full of air-bubbles, bumps, flaws and irregularities which break up the sun's rays, make the light split into colors and the glass sparkle. This vibrating, shining, dancing, refracted light is the glory of the stained glass windows of the twelfth and thirteenth centuries. The beauty of these panes is further enhanced by the great number of pieces composing them, which interrupt the colors: 350 to 450 pieces to a square meter have been counted.

In spite of its hardness, the glass has sometimes been attacked by lichens which have pierced it from the outside in numerous little pits and caused whitish spots. Certain colors, notably white, rose, purple and yellow, have suffered particularly. But the stained glass window has no patina in the true sense of the word. Dust and the decomposition of lead and putty have occasionally dulled the glass, but the colors have remained intact and a cleaning suffices to restore the window to its original luster.

The glass-painter, with his palette of plain and colored pieces of glass on hand, makes the cartoon or working-drawing of the window, always very simple in design. The lines of the drawing and the silhouettes of the characters are strongly marked and the draperies clearly indicated; but even though the figures are frankly isolated on the background, they none the less remain incorporated in it. They never seem to protrude from the pane; there is neither perspective nor an attempt to bring the figures into relief. The stained glass window, like a tapestry, is not supposed to make a gap in the wall, but is part of the decorative scheme of the bay. The upper windows usually contained a single figure, or a simple, easily recognizable scene; the narrative panes belonged to the lower windows, and the scenes, fitted into medallions, usually read from left to right, starting at the bottom. After the end of the twelfth and during the thirteenth centuries, the lower parts often held likenesses of the donors: nobles, clergy, rich notables, guilds and corporations shown at their work.

During the twelfth and early thirteenth centuries, the medallions were frequently linked by a background of palm leaves, foliage, bouquets and stylized leaves, of which the wide borders were also composed. Around 1220, it became the custom to save time by adorning the background simply with lattice-work of a square, lozenge, circular, or fish-scale pattern executed in reds and blues. The abuse of this practice in the second half of the thirteenth century often gave the whole a rather chilly purple effect. The borders, narrower now, were frequently decorated only with heraldic devices or juxtaposed geometric motifs.

The stained glass window has considerable educational value, as M. Mâle has so well brought out in his books. The window was not only a decoration, a magnificent decoration which gives the inside of our cathedrals that warm, living, opalescent atmosphere which we admire at Chartres, Bourges, or in the Sainte-Chapelle; it was also a means of instruction, and in those Gothic churches where windows more and more took the place of walls, occupying all the free space between the piers supporting the arches, stained glass filled the role which, from early Christian times to the end of the Roman era, was occupied by mosaics and murals. Suger in the twelfth century and Jean Gerson at the beginning of the fifteenth asserted: 'The images in the church windows are put there for no other purpose than to show simple folk ignorant of the Scriptures what they ought to believe.' And M. René Couffon recently cited this passage from an old catechism of the diocese of Trequier, where to the question, 'What should one do upon entering a cathedral?' the answer reads: 'Take holy water, adore the Blessed Sacrament, then walk all around the edifice and look at the stained glass windows.'

In the upper windows one finds Christ and the Virgin, sometimes accompanied by angels and archangels. The patriarchs, prophets, and patron saints of the church are generally placed on the north side;

corresponding to these on the south side are the apostles, martyrs, and great saints of Christianity, those whose relics were owned by the church or who were especially honored in the diocese. Sometimes there were placed in the apse, as at Poitiers and Lyons, scenes of the Passion, Resurrection, and Ascension of Christ, evoked by the prayer 'Suscipe' in the Mass, whence the clergy derived the general idea for the iconography of many of the churches.

The medallions of the lower windows set forth the story of Christ, the Virgin, the apostles, martyrs, and saints, and also depict the symbols of the Old and New Testaments (whose 'concordance' is everywhere affirmed, the Old Testament heralding and foreshadowing the New), the parables of the gospel, signs of the zodiac, the 'occupations of the months' and the 'battles of virtues and vices.' Sometimes, as in the Sainte-Chapelle in Paris, the entire story of the Bible is chronicled in pictures.

In the time of Theophilus, the silhouettes, costumes, details, and color divisions were drawn on a wooden table coated with whitewash; later on they were cut out in parchment, wooden boards, or thin sheets of metal. The pieces of glass were set up on the model and cut with a red-hot iron, the rough edges being clipped off with pliers called grozing irons.

The same cartoon was sometimes used for several figures, as in the upper windows of the choirs of Bourges and St. Père of Chartres, in the transept of Chartres Cathedral, or in the windows of the arch of Jesse in the Sainte-Chapelle in Paris. Occasionally entire scenes are traced from the same design, such as those of the Coronation of the King in the window of Numbers in the Sainte-Chapelle. But the difference in color precludes monotony, and these resemblances are apparent only to the most observant spectator, so predominant is the color of these ancient windows over their design.

When the glass had been assembled as required on the cartoon, the glass-craftsman traced the features, details, folds of garments, shadows, and general design with a paint or enamel known as *grisaille*— a mixture that during the Middle Ages consisted of copper filings, iron shavings, and powdered glass ground up in vinegar, oil or gum. The paint, of a warm gray-brown tint, was put on with a brush in broad or slender strokes, or in a thin layer that was allowed to dry, and was then removed where clear spaces were required to represent hair, beard, modeling and shadows. These shadings were also obtained by means of close strokes or hatchings traced with a brush. The inscriptions were generally executed in clear letters on a black background. These are easier to read in transparency than letters in black on a clear background, which at a distance would be obliterated by the light. For the same reason, figures were outlined in a strongly marked, sometimes almost caricatured design, so that they might retain their value when silhouetted against the sun's rays. The *grisaille*, put on in a thin coat with clear areas revealing the pure colors here and there, was also used to give the colors their value, to subdue those which would have been too strident, to fill in those which would have made a gap, and to reduce the intensity of certain hues, notably the blues, which would otherwise have encroached upon other colors. At the end of the thirteenth century, in order to subdue their excessive brilliance, the backgrounds were filled in with arabesques designed in *grisaille* which were later outlined with hard brushes and the aid of a stencil-plate in a thin layer of the same *grisaille*.

Once the paint was applied, the glass was put into the furnace, and during fusion the color penetrated and became absorbed into the mixture.

In the twelfth and thirteenth centuries, this completed the making of the glass. The numerous pieces were again placed upon the model for mounting. They were assembled in leadings with wide, high cores, and thick, short flanges that accommodated the various thicknesses of the glass. These leadings were cast in a mold; some of them, according to M. Chesnau, were formed, after the thirteenth century, by grooving on a wheel. They were joined together by soldering. The purpose of the leadings was not only to keep the pieces of glass in place; they also served by their broad dark lines to accentuate the silhouettes, figures, draped folds, and various details of the garments, and also to separate certain tones whose juxtaposition would interfere with the harmony of color. The Cistercians, who were forbidden by law

8

to use colored glass, have solely by means of leadings and *grisaille* composed very fine colorless windows of a highly decorative design.

The complete stained glass window consists of a number of panels of from 60 to 80 centimeters set between iron crossbars and held in place by small rods, formerly square but now round, about which were tied leaden ribbons soldered to the leading of the windows. The panels are secured by catches or bolts fastened to the crossbars by means of pegs; they were formerly held in place by a key of mortar or putty. Rods, catches, and pegs are always placed on the side from which it is easiest to reach the windows, generally on the outer supporting cornice for the upper windows, and on the inside for the lower windows. In the twelfth century, and at the beginning of the thirteenth, the vertical and horizontal iron bars cross each other at right angles for the upper windows, making a series of frames which enclose the panels. From the thirteenth century on, the bars of the lower windows were shaped by blacksmiths to form lozenges, circular medallions, semicircles, quatrefoils, and large-petaled, beautifully formed flowers, to the shapes of which the panels were adapted. It is interesting to note the close resemblance between certain armatures in different cathedrals, at Chartres and Bourges for example. This resemblance is so evident that one wonders if the blacksmiths did not accompany the glass-workers in their travels from place to place. About 1220 or 1230, for the upper windows, and a little later for the lower, stone mullions with small arches surmounted by roses were introduced, and windows that were too broad to give the glass sufficient support were divided into lancets and tracery patterns. During the twelfth, and even in the thirteenth century, in many churches such as the cathedrals of Rheims and Chartres, the windows were mounted in wooden frames set into the rabbet of the stone frame; and after the thirteenth century, it seems to have been the custom to fit the glass into the rabbet or groove by means of clay and plaster keys.

The people of the Middle Ages so cherished these windows, where the lives of Christ, the Virgin, and the saints were unfolded against an azure sky, that in spite of the destruction of time and changes in style—many were replaced in the eighteenth century by a white lozenged glass—in spite of revolutions and restorations, a great number of them are still in existence.

We have hardly any stained glass windows prior to the middle of the twelfth century. The windows of St. Denis may be considered as among the most ancient: they probably date back to the dedication of the choir in 1144 or to the years immediately following. A large number of them were destroyed during the Revolution, and several fragments were collected by Lenoir, who used them to decorate the Museum of French Monuments; from here they were taken by the Gérentes, and, under the supervision of Viollet-le-Duc and Baron de Guilhermy, reset in the chapels of the choir tower of St. Denis.

Suger, the great abbot of St. Denis, who died in 1151, speaks with enthusiasm in his *Livre sur son administration* of the windows which he had constructed to educate the people and to 'direct thought by material means toward that which is immaterial.' He had artists come from afar, and sparing no efforts, himself prescribed the subjects, directed the execution, and charged a master-specialist with the preservation of the windows. The congregation, moreover, had such an admiration for these windows, he tells us, that the collection-box placed in the church for their maintenance was always full.

Among those windows which it was possible to replace and restore more or less completely at St. Denis, special mention should be made of the window of the Griffons, reminiscent in composition and coloring of the most sumptuous Oriental rugs, and the two windows of the life of Moses and the Concordance of the Old and New Testaments in the north chapel, opening off the center chapel. The latter contains a little portrait of Suger prostrate at the feet of the Virgin of the Annunciation, and the Tree of Jesse, conceived after the text of the prophecy of Isaiah: from the extended body of Jesse rises the mighty tree whose branches bear the royal ancestors of the Virgin and Christ, portrayed at the top, while along the sides ascend the prophets who from age to age proclaimed His coming.

9

I

The three windows of the western façade of Chartres cathedral belong to the same school. They were made at the same time as the statues of the Portail Royal, in the middle of the twelfth century, and were also moved to their present places after the fire of 1194. In composition, technique, and coloring, as well as in many details of their execution, they can be likened to the ancient windows of St. Denis. To the right is shown the Tree of Jesse. In the center, the life of Christ from the Annunciation to the Entry into Jerusalem is pictured in twenty-nine panels, alternately round and square, with blue and red backgrounds which in themselves constitute an immense checkerboard of color. To the left are depicted in fourteen round medallions the scenes of the Passion and the Resurrection of Christ. At the top of the central window the Virgin holding the Child is enthroned in majesty, in the style of the miraculous Virgin of Chartres, often repeated in the windows of the cathedral.

One of these Virgins, also dating from the twelfth century, was saved from the fire of 1194 and remounted in the thirteenth century in the south side of the choir; this is Notre-Dame de la Belle-Verrière.

She well deserves her name. Seated in full face, holding straight before her the Child with His hands raised in blessing, in her beautiful clear blue robe, her head encircled with an equally blue halo, she stands out in unforgettable harmony against a great red background sown with blue stars. In the thirteenth century she was framed in a border of angels kneeling upon a blue ground, very different from the twelfth century blues, whose pure beauty may be seen in the windows of the western façade. Those thousand pieces of glass, kindled by the setting sun at close of day, sparkle like jewels and illuminate the great structure with their brilliant hues.

The influence of the workshops of Chartres and St. Denis is shown in other stained glass windows of the middle and third quarter of the twelfth century which are still found in certain churches and cathedrals of western France, notably those of St. Stephen, St. Gervais, and St. Protais in Mans; and in the windows showing the passion of St. Catherine, the death of the Virgin, and the legend of St. Vincent on the north side of the nave of the cathedral of Angers, all given by the cantor Hugues de Chamblancé. In 1850 Henri Gérente, looking at the windows of the cathedral of Mans, came upon the beautiful fragment of the Ascension showing the Virgin between two groups of three apostles, and below, three groups of two apostles, magnificent figures upon alternate red and blue backgrounds. These may be considered as forerunners of the stained glass of Poitiers.

The great bay window of the flat apse of the cathedral of Poitiers, eight meters high and three wide, is adorned with a magnificent window, the date of which has been much discussed. Its composition, iconographic details, design, and coloring, and also technique, all point to the second half of the twelfth century, despite the conclusions drawn from an inscription, almost illegible before the restoration of the glass by Steinbeil in the nineteenth century. Here some claim to read the name of the Blason family who, despoiled by the Plantagenets, did not recover their property until after the victory of the King of France in 1204. This would make the window date back to the beginning of the thirteenth century.

The center of the bay is dominated by a monumental figure of Christ upon the cross, flanked by the Virgin and St. John, Longinus and Stephaton, on a red ground bordered in blue. Below, the holy women contemplate the empty tomb shown them by the Angel. Above, the risen Christ in a red aureole ascends to heaven in the presence of the Virgin and apostles, accompanied by the figures of two angels whose bodies, exactly filling the space between the aureole of Christ and the border of the window, form extraordinary arabesques such as are found in the Burgundian tympans of Roman sculptors.

One might also mention several other stained glass windows of the twelfth century—at St. Denis de Jouhet in the Indre, at Champs near Grenoble, where Bégule has commented on three panels representing the Pentecost and the Ascension; and also at St. Remi in Rheims, in the cathedral of Châlons-sur-Marne (today in the Museum of French Monuments), in the cathedral of Metz, and in several churches of Alsace and of Lorraine. As M. Mâle has shown, these windows of Champagne and the East display certain characteristics different from those of the St. Denis and Chartres family: backgrounds often uncolored or green, sometimes of concentric panes, Carolingian survivals in iconography, a wealth of inscriptions, and frequent use of a beautiful green as startling as emerald, for example, in the window of St. Paul in the south transept of Metz cathedral.

In the thirteenth century the windows became larger and the stained glass covered increasingly greater surfaces. The technique is still that of the twelfth century, as we have described it in St. Denis and Chartres. Certain tones were slightly altered, such as the blues which tended at times to purple, at times to green; the others remain practically the same. The red backgrounds gradually lost their vogue in favor of blue ones patterned in lozenges, squares, or lattice-work. Some changes were made in the style of design. As in painting, miniatures, and sculpture, the figures were no longer elongated in clinging vestments which outlined the forms of the bodies; the proportions became more realistic and the figures were draped in loose garments which followed their gestures and attitudes. The curious resemblance between all these thirteenth century stained glass windows has often been noted. Certain great workshops set the pattern for what we find at Chartres, Sens, Bourges, Laon, and Rouen, and they doubtless executed the great windows of Notre-Dame in Paris, and later those in the Sainte-Chapelle. In these shops were trained the glass-painters who were later to work all over France. Only one has signed his work—one of the stained windows in the choir of Rouen cathedral. His name was Clement and he was a native of Chartres, and we thus understand the kinship of the windows of the ambulatory at Rouen with those of the ambulatory of Chartres.

Immediately after the burning of the old cathedral of Chartres in 1194, the reconstruction of the new cathedral was begun: the nave was built first, then the choir, then the upper parts of the transept. The stained glass windows were made at the same time. The glass-painters, who probably came to Paris at the end of the twelfth century, returned to Chartres immediately after the disaster, and during the first thirty years of the thirteenth century, designed 173 windows covering a surface of more than two thousand square meters. Canon Y. Delaporte, who has analyzed these windows in a very fine book illustrated with the photographs of Ét. Houvet, shows that they may be divided into three groups: the windows of the nave and aisles; those of the choir, the ambulatory, and the chapels that opened out from it; and those of the upper windows of the transept. Possibly they all are the work of the same shops, executed in three different regions, or the work of different shops but similar in construction, having been made at three successive stages as the work progressed. These windows were donated by the congregation—sixteen by the clergy, forty-four by kings and nobles, forty-two by guilds and corporations; the others have not been identified. No definite plan for the whole is discernible except that the windows of the apse are consecrated to the Virgin, the north rose to the triumph of Mary, and the south rose to the triumph of Christ, thus repeating the symbolic idea which regulated the decoration of the portals below. The upper windows are filled with great isolated figures—the Virgin, apostles, martyrs, saints; the lower windows with legendary scenes taken from the Old and New Testaments, whose concordance is asserted in a striking manner in the clerestory under the rose of the south transept, where we see the four great prophets bearing the four Evangelists on their shoulders. The windows of the nave, which are the oldest, may date from about 1205 to 1215; those of the choir, from 1215 to 1225; and those of the ambulatory and the radiating chapels from perhaps 1230. The rose of the north transept, above the great figures of the clerestory, which are among the most beautiful in existence, was presented by the Royal House of France between 1223 and 1234; the rose of the south transept between 1212 and 1226 by the House of Dreux-Bretagne.

No other cathedral possesses such a wealth of stained glass windows and they give it that uniquely mellow, iridescent atmosphere, bluer in cloudy weather, more red and orange on sunny days. Chartres should be visited either in the morning or the evening if its full beauty is to be comprehended—in the morning when the sun kindles in the windows of the apse those never-dying flames (an expression used by the vine-dressers of Mans in giving a window to their cathedral); in the evening, when the slanting rays of the setting sun make the deep blues of the west façade and the brilliant reds of the heavenly figures in the north transept sparkle like rare stones. The lofty windows of the west façade fade out, dusk descends upon the great nave, then suddenly the rose of the north façade, kindled by a last ray of the sun, flares forth in incomparable splendor. The inimitable jewels then gradually grow dull, and everything recedes into the tranquil peace of that twilight that the hundred windows of the cathedral never allow to sink into utter night.

The four medallion windows of the north side and of the ambulatory of the cathedral of Sens, although sometimes attributed to the late twelfth century, should be dated early thirteenth. The armature designs, the details of composition and iconography, and the colors, all tend to the same conclusion. They are of exceptional merit, and one of them, the window of the parable of the Good Samaritan (which is also to be found in Chartres and Bourges), surpasses the others in the harmony of its composition as well as in the decorative value of its execution. The others are devoted to the parable of the Prodigal Son, and to the stories of St. Eustache and St. Thomas à Becket.

Very similar to the windows of Sens and Chartres are those of the apse of Laon cathedral, and those of the choir of Bourges where some of the Chartres workshops probably operated—notably the narrative windows of the second ambulatory and the little chapels opening off from it, done probably around 1220. Here should be noted as among the most beautiful, those of the New Alliance, of the Passion, the Last Judgment, the Good Samaritan, and the Prodigal Son, St. Stephen, St. Nicholas, St. Mary the Egyptian, St. Mary Magdalen, etc. Likenesses of the bishops of Bourges are placed in the windows of the first ambulatory on either side of the Virgin and Christ. The stained glass of the upper windows of the choir, made perhaps a few years later, show, in the apse, the Virgin between St. John the Baptist and St. Stephen, patron saint of the cathedral; then, on the north side, prophets and patriarchs; and on the south side, apostles and evangelists—extraordinary figures, so well constructed, so strongly outlined, that, despite the great height at which they are placed, they still retain in the rays of the sun a memorable dramatic beauty and power.

The influence of the stained glass of Chartres and Bourges is still to be found in the first half of the thirteenth century at Poitiers, Rouen, Lyon (although here the iconography and style vary somewhat), in many smaller churches, and in the Sainte-Chapelle at Paris, the windows of which were completed at its dedication in 1248, as Mrs. Jeannette Dyer Spencer has proved. From there the style spread rapidly throughout France, sometimes hasty in execution, but here and there nobly successful, as at Soissons, Amiens and Rheims, at Coutances, Tours, Le Mans and Angers, at Auxerre, and at Clermont-Ferrand. The trellised backgrounds grew in number, the architectural framework developed, medallions often replaced the large figures, while geometric designs and rather severe combinations of lines supplanted the palm leaves and lush foliage, and sometimes even the figures and scenes. But the decorative feeling persisted as vividly as ever, as may be seen in the beautiful rose window which, with its double tier of figures below, has since the beginning of the fourteenth century been illuminating the end of the north transept of the cathedral of Amiens.

The stained glass window was to develop, change in some of its aspects, and use some new technical processes, but it was yet to know three centuries of splendor.

MARCEL AUBERT
Member of the Institute

PLATES

(Translator's Note: The dimensions of these windows are given in meters and centimeters. A meter is 1.093633 yards and the centimeter, the hundredth part of a meter, is 0.39371 inch.)

I. *Text.*—Cathedral of Bourges. Upper windows of choir; north side.—The prophets Micheas and Jonas.—First half of the 13th century. Micheas: Height, 4,23, Width, 1,15; Jonas: H. 4,24, W. 1,21.

II. *Text.*—Cathedral of Bourges. Upper windows of choir, north side.—The prophets Amos and Nahum.—First half of the 13th century. Amos: H. 4,23, W. 1,25; Nahum: H. 4,21, W. 1,14.

III.—Cathedral of Le Mans. Second window of the south aisle.—Fragments of the Ascension.—Middle of the 12th century. H. 1,79, W. 1,30.

IV.—Cathedral of Chartres. First window of the choir aisle, south side. Notre-Dame de la Belle-Verrière. Middle of the 12th century. H. 4,90, W. 2,36.

V.—Cathedral of Chartres. Central window of the west facade, lower panels.—The Annunciation, the Visitation, the Nativity, the Tidings to the shepherds, Herod and his councillors, the Magi.—Middle of the 12th century. H. 1,80, W. 2,72.

VI.—Cathedral of Poitiers. Window of the apse.—Crucifixion, Resurrection and Ascension.—Second half of the 12th century. H. 6,45, W. 3,00.

VII.—Cathedral of Sens. Window in the north choir aisle.—Story of St. Thomas à Becket, seven lower medallions: Reconciliation of St. Thomas and Henry II of England through the mediation of Louis VII; St. Thomas lands in England; he makes his entrance into Canterbury; he is received by the monks; he preaches from the rood-loft; he celebrates Mass; he receives a letter from the king.—Beginning of the 13th century. H. 3,04, W. 2,45.

VIII.—Cathedral of Sens. Window of the ambulatory, north side.—Detail of the window of the Good Samaritan; the traveler is attacked by brigands; Adam and Eve are expelled from the earthly paradise by the archangel.—Beginning of the 13th century. H. 1,05, W. 0,73.

IX.—Cathedral of Chartres. Fourth window in the south aisle of the nave.—Lower medallion of the window devoted to the Death, the Burial and Assumption of the Virgin, given by the shoemakers: the Death of the Virgin.—Beginning of the 13th century. H. 1,90, W. 1,38.

X.—Cathedral of Chartres. Third window of the north aisle of the nave. Detail of the window of St. Eustace, given by the drapers and furriers: St. Eustace kneeling before the miraculous stag. 'Placidas' was the name of the saint before his baptism.—Beginning of the 13th century. H. 1,43, W. 1,04.

XI.—Cathedral of Chartres. Third window of the south aisle of the nave. Central part of the window of the Good Samaritan, given by the shoemakers: the wounded man is bound up by the Good Samaritan, conducted by him to the inn, where the inn-keeper attends him; above he is in bed and the inn-keeper lavishes care upon him. In the same four-leaf design: to the left, the Creation of Adam; in the center, Adam in the earthly paradise; to the right, the Creation of Eve; above, Adam and Eve near the tree of knowledge of good and evil.—First quarter of the 13th century. H. 2,89, W. 2,00.

XII.—Cathedral of Chartres. Third south window of the nave. The Virgin with the Child Jesus between the donors; below, the Apparition of Christ to Magdalen.—First quarter of the 13th century. H. 6,88, W. 2,17.

Second south window of the nave.—St. James; below the donors—bakers and pastry-makers.—First quarter of the 13th century. H. 7,27, W. 1,89.

XIII.—Cathedral of Chartres. Window of the apse, to the left of the center window.—Angel bearing censer; window given by Geoffroy of the shoemakers' guild.—First third of the 13th century. H. 7,15, W. 2,18.

XIV.—Cathedral of Chartres. Central portion of the great lancets under the rose of the north transept. St. Ann holding the Virgin; beneath her the shield of France, azure strewn with fleurs-de-lis. She is shown between David playing his ten-stringed harp, standing above Saul who is piercing himself with his sword after the disaster of Gelboe, and Solomon standing above Jeroboam who is kneeling before two golden calves.—The rose and the clerestory were given by the House of France in the reign of Blanche of Castille, 1223-1226, or during her regency, 1226-1236. David: H. 7,45, W. 1,55; St. Ann: H. 7,47, W. 1,70; Solomon: H. 7,44, W. 1,57.

XV.—Cathedral of Bourges. Ambulatory window to the right of the central apsidal chapel.—Lower part of the window of the Prodigal Son: below the donors, tanners at their work; above, the Prodigal Son asking his father for his share of the inheritance; to the left, he is receiving his money, to the right he leaves on horseback, while in the center his brother is tilling the soil; he then meets a courtesan; above he is welcomed and feasted by the courtesans; upper right, he is being driven out, despoiled of everything.—First quarter of the 13th century. H. 2,52, W. 1,85.

XVI.—Cathedral of Bourges. Ambulatory window south of the axis.—Center part of the window of the Passion: the Pharisees try to ensnare Christ in his own words; they bargain with Judas; the Last Supper; Washing of the Feet; Resurrection of Lazarus; Agony of Jesus in the Garden of Olives; the Money-changers driven out of the Temple.—First quarter of the 13th century. H. 1,25, W. 1,90.

XVII.—Cathedral of Bourges. Upper windows of the apse, south side.—St. Peter and St. Paul; St. John.—First half of the 13th century. St. Peter: H. 4,45, W. 1,08; St. Paul: H. 4,46, W. 1,09; St. John: H. 4,43, W. 1,02.

XVIII.—Cathedral of Amiens. Rose and lancets below in the north transept.—Beginning of the 14th century. H. 20,40, W. 11,50.

XIX. *Front.*—Cathedral of Bourges. Ambulatory window to the south of the axis chapel.—Upper part of the window of the Last Judgment, given perhaps by the priests of the cathedral: in the center, Christ judging; at his feet, the Virgin and St. John representing God's pity; on either side angels carrying the lance and the cross, representing God's justice; below, the apostles; above, the angels; at the top, the dove and seven crowned figures—the seven gifts of the Holy Ghost.—First quarter of the 13th century. H. 2,60, W. 1,90.

The plates in this volume were made, with the aid of perfected photographic processes, directly from the originals; moreover, each plate has been verified before the windows themselves.

The editors wish to thank the French autorities, especially the Ministry of Beaux-Arts and the chief architects, as well as the local and ecclesiastical authorities, for their kindness in facilitating their work.

The choice of plates and the direction of the work of photographing and reproduction was carried out by Dr. H. Zbinden of Berne.

The measurements, in meters and centimeters, are taken from the edges of the stained glass windows (omitting the stone or iron framework), and, for the details, represent the exact dimensions of the sections reproduced.

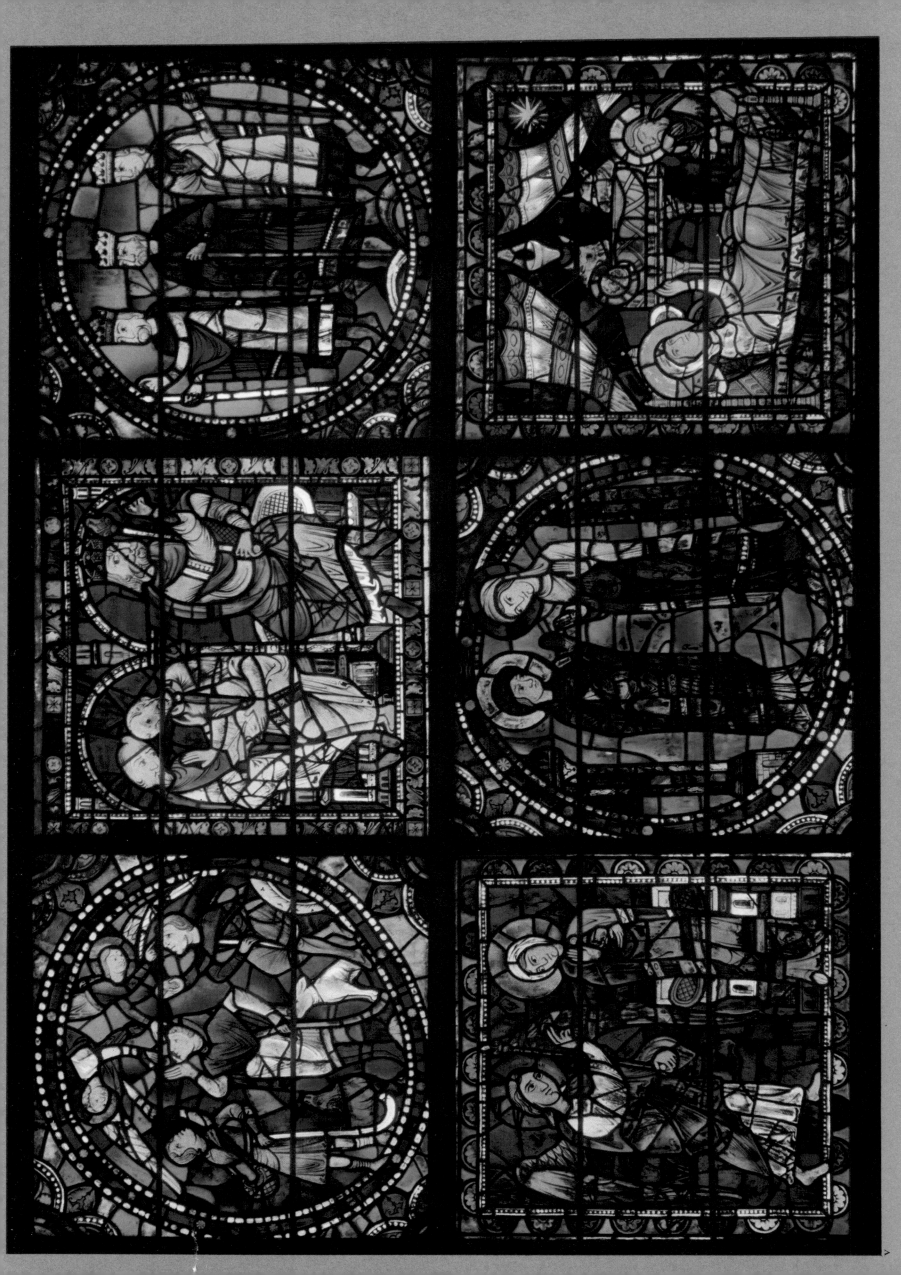

VII

IX

XIII